HARRIET TUBMAN AND MY GRANDMOTHER'S QUILTS

LORENZO PACE

WINDMILL BOOKS

New York

Published in 2015 by The Rosen Publishing Group, Inc.
29 East 21st Street, New York, NY 10010

First Edition

Book Design: Brian Garvey

All artwork by Lorenzo Pace

Library of Congress Cataloging-in-Publication Data

Pace, Lorenzo.
Harriet Tubman and my grandmother's quilts / by Lorenzo Pace.
p. cm. — (African American quartet)
ISBN 978-1-4777-9289-6 (library binding) — ISBN 978-1-4777-9290-2 (pbk.) — ISBN 978-1-4777-9291-9 (6-pack)
1. Tubman, Harriet, — 1820?–1913 — Juvenile literature. 2. African American abolitionists — Juvenile literature. 3. Underground Railroad — Juvenile literature. I. Pace, Lorenzo. II. Title.
E444.T82 P334 2015
973.7—d23

Manufactured in the United States of America

Cover and interior pages (quilts), pp. 43, 47 Cindy Reiman; pp. 5, 45 courtesy of the author. Image sources: p. 7 Hulton Archive/Archive Photos/Getty Images; p. 9 File:AfricanSlavesTransport.jpg/Wikimedia Commons; p. 17 Mansell/Time Life Pictures/Getty Images; p. 21 (top) The Washington Post/Getty Images; p. 21 (bottom) New York Daily News/Getty Images; p. 23 MPI/Archive Photos/Getty Images; p. 27 © AP Images; p. 29 (bottom) File:Undergroundrailroadsmall2jpg/Wikimedia Commons; pp. 29 (top), 37 (left) Library of Congress Prints and Photographs Division; p. 31 U.S. National Park Service; p. 33 Universal Images Group/Getty Images; p. 33 (inset) File:1852 Picayune Slaves.jpg/Wikimedia Commons; p. 35 David Redfern/Redferns/Getty Images; p. 39 Ira Block/ National Geographic Image Collection/Getty Images; p. 41 © iStockphoto.com/cgering

Harriet Tubman and My Grandmother's Quilts

More than one hundred years ago, my grandmother made quilts for our family. She used old clothes, food sacks, and anything else she could find. She turned worn-out things into something beautiful.

4

5

When I was a little boy, she told me stories about a woman named Harriet Tubman. My grandmother was only 74 years younger than Harriet. My grandmother could understand how hard Harriet's life had been.

7

In 1822, Harriet Tubman was born in Maryland. Her parents were slaves, and so Harriet was a slave, too. Slaves were brought by force from Africa to work without pay. They were bought and sold like property. They had no rights or freedom.

When Harriet was a little girl, she worked with her family for long hours in the fields picking cotton, potatoes, and peanuts. It was hard work.

11

When I was growing up in Alabama in the 1940s, I also worked in the fields with my mother and my entire family. We were farmers. Unlike Harriet, we were able to rent our land.

13

When Harriet was 22 years old, she married John Tubman, a freeman. But she remained a slave, and in October 1849, Harriet decided to escape. She was never a slave in her mind.

Slaves were at great risk in trying to escape from their owners. If caught, they could be killed.

17

Harriet was very brave. She escaped at night. Other brave people helped her find a secret route to freedom. This route was called the Underground Railroad.

19

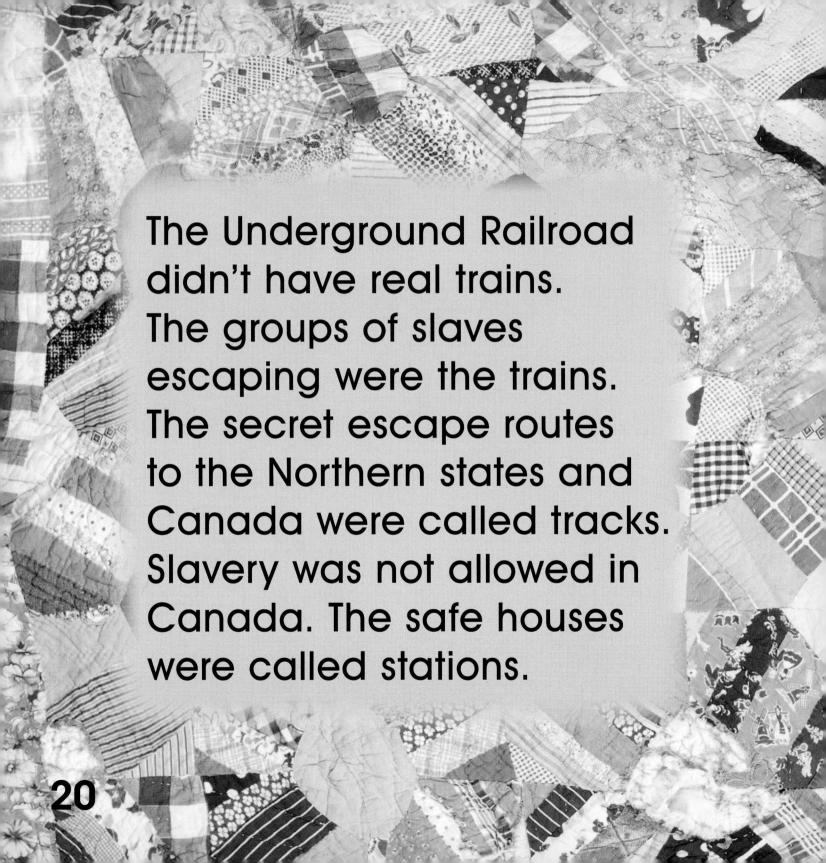

The Underground Railroad didn't have real trains. The groups of slaves escaping were the trains. The secret escape routes to the Northern states and Canada were called tracks. Slavery was not allowed in Canada. The safe houses were called stations.

21

Harriet escaped to freedom, and in 1849, she arrived in Pennsylvania. She found a job, worked very hard, and saved every penny she could. Harriet was free, but she wanted the rest of her family to be free as well!

23

She used the money she had saved to travel to Baltimore. She helped stop her niece from being sold. A few months later, Harriet returned to Baltimore and helped other slaves escape. Harriet continued to make many dangerous trips at night to help more slaves find freedom.

In 1854, Harriet became a "conductor," or guide, on the Underground Railroad. There were many routes of the Underground Railroad. But all went from the South to the North. I live in Brooklyn near one of the famous stations. It is now a museum that people can visit. There are many stations that are now museums along the old routes of the Underground Railroad.

After my grandmother and mother died, I was given all the quilts they had made. Some people say the pictures in the quilts gave directions to the slaves escaping along the Underground Railroad. Some say this is not true. I don't know.

ROUTES OF THE
UNDERGROUND
RAILROAD
1830 - 1865

Compiled from "The Underground Railroad from
Slavery to Freedom" By Wilbur H. Siebert.
Copyright, 1898, by The Macmillan Company.

29

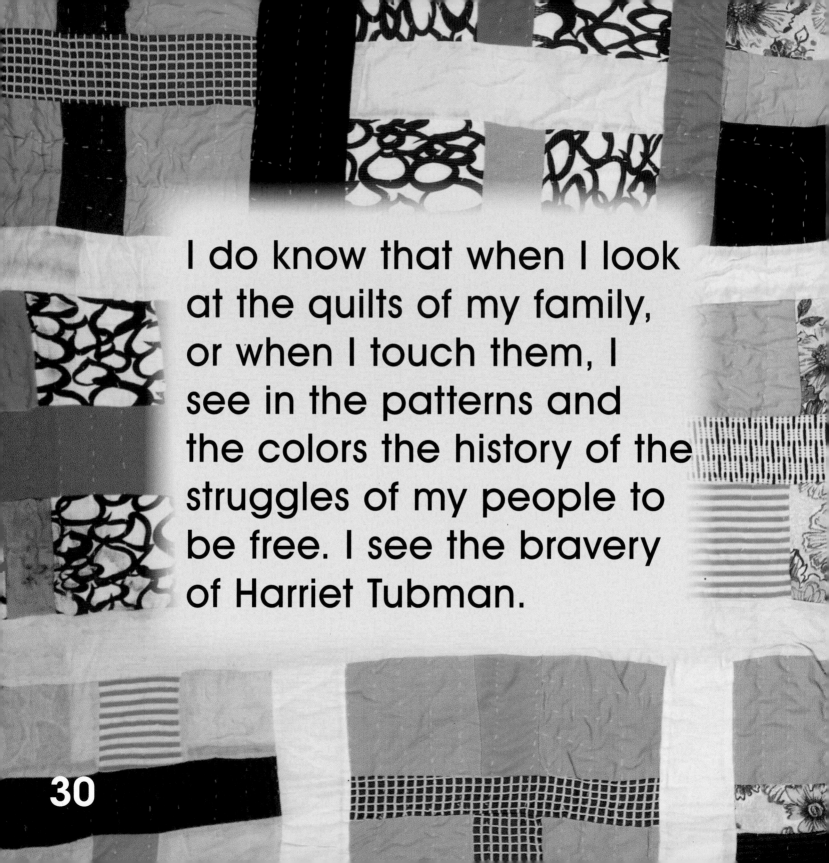

I do know that when I look at the quilts of my family, or when I touch them, I see in the patterns and the colors the history of the struggles of my people to be free. I see the bravery of Harriet Tubman.

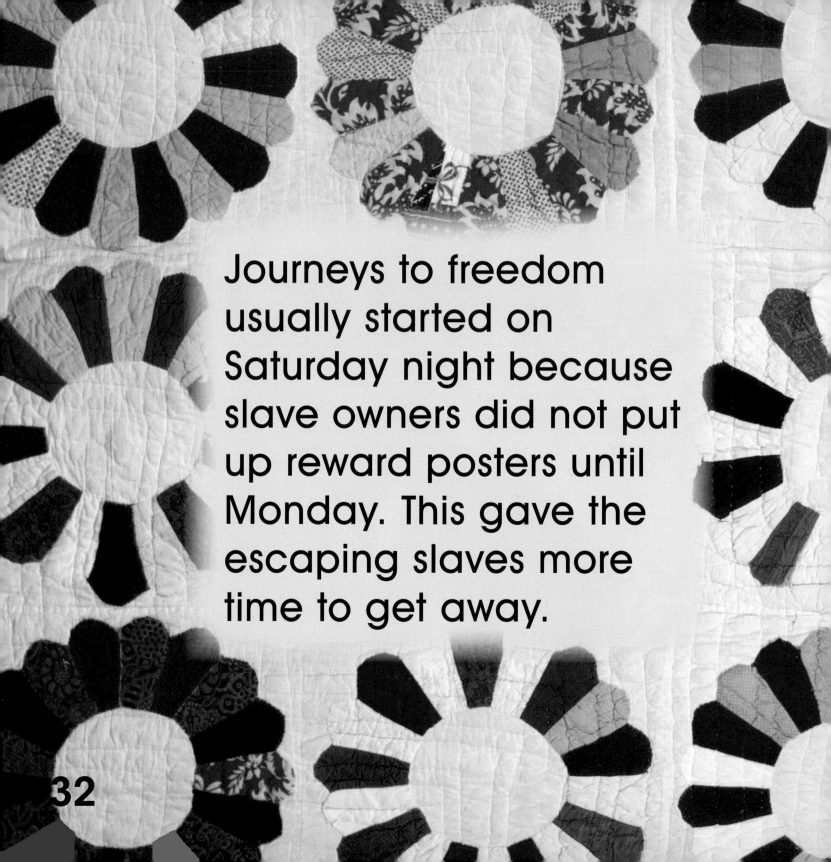

Journeys to freedom usually started on Saturday night because slave owners did not put up reward posters until Monday. This gave the escaping slaves more time to get away.

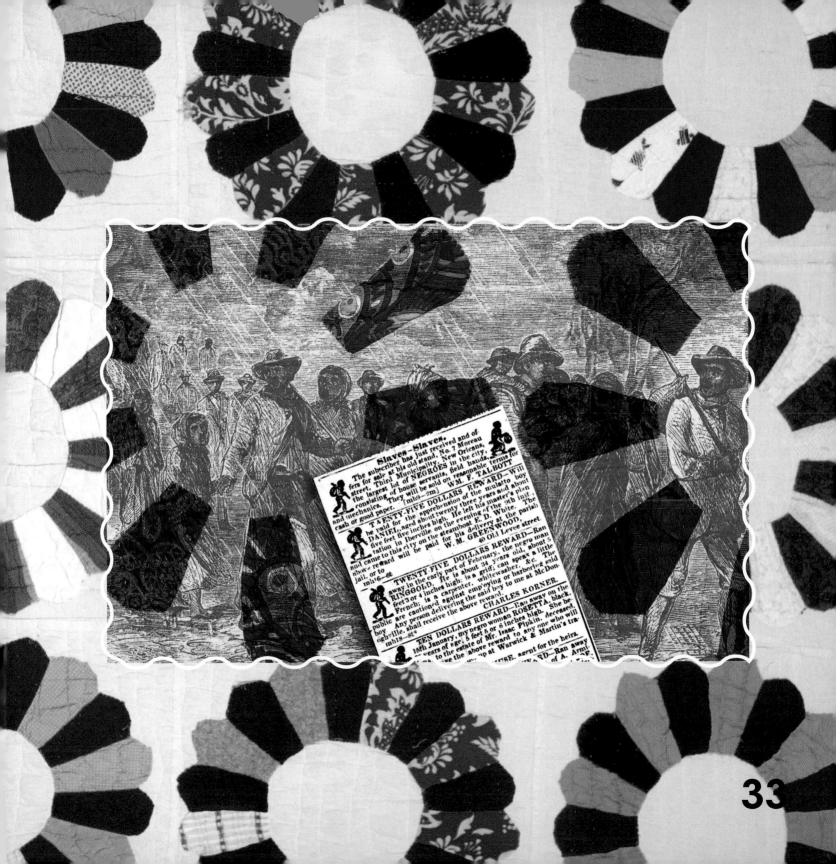

33

When Harriet led an escape, she often sang a spiritual to let slaves know it was safe to begin the journey. We still sing some of these same spirituals today.

35

Harriet Tubman helped more than 300 slaves escape to freedom. She also became a soldier and nurse for the Union Army during the Civil War. The Civil War was fought between the Northern free states and the Southern slave-owning states. The war lasted five years, from 1861 to 1865. The North won the war and all slaves became free.

37

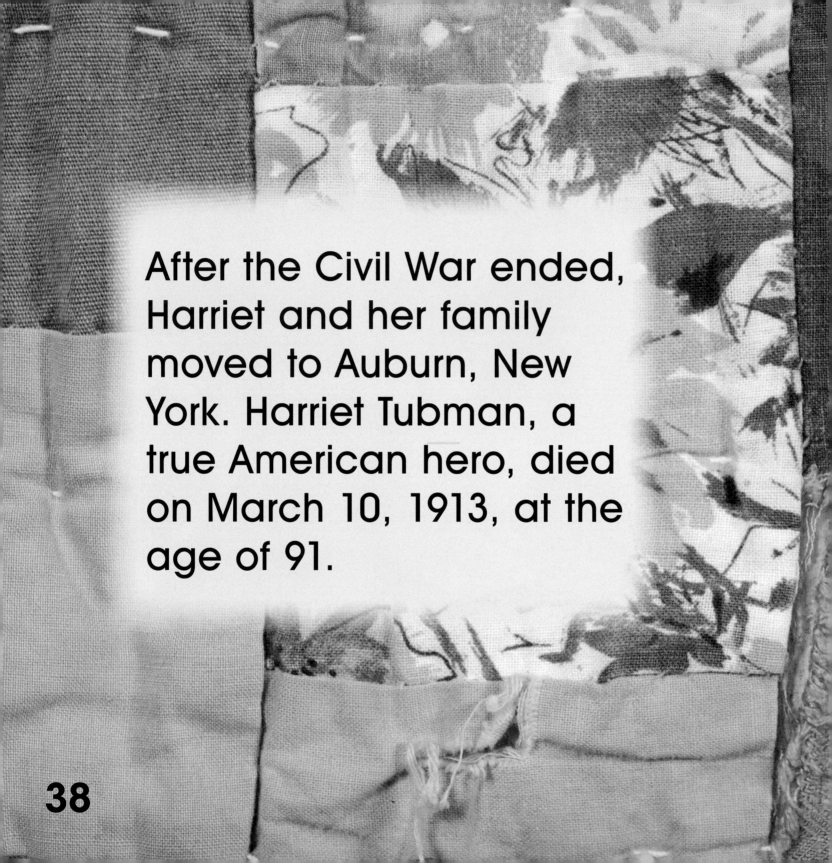

After the Civil War ended, Harriet and her family moved to Auburn, New York. Harriet Tubman, a true American hero, died on March 10, 1913, at the age of 91.

39

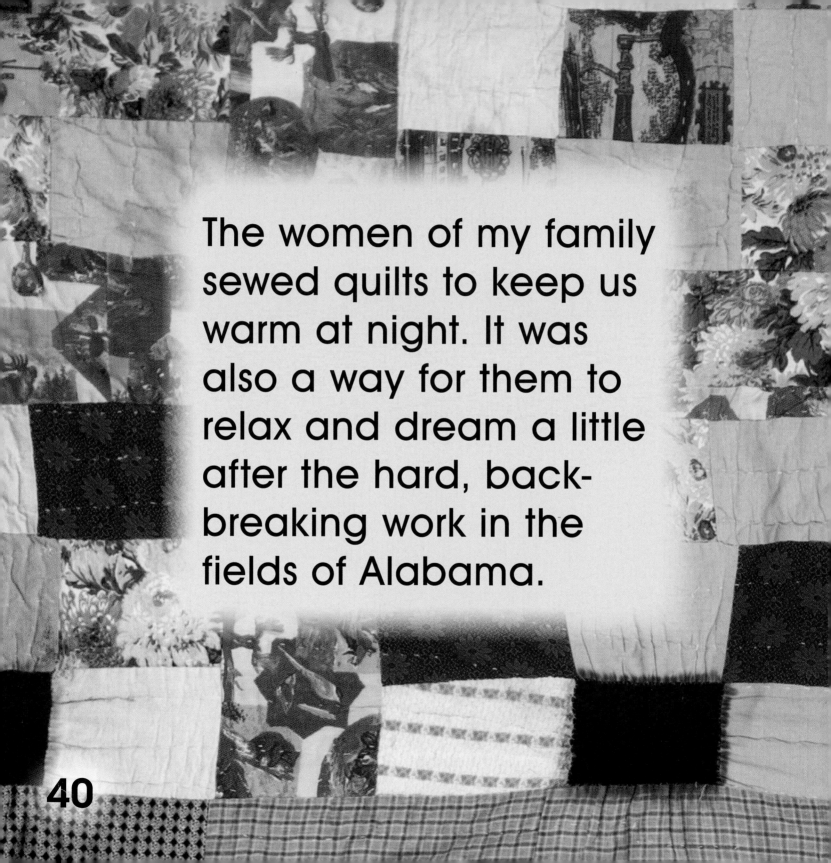

The women of my family sewed quilts to keep us warm at night. It was also a way for them to relax and dream a little after the hard, back-breaking work in the fields of Alabama.

41

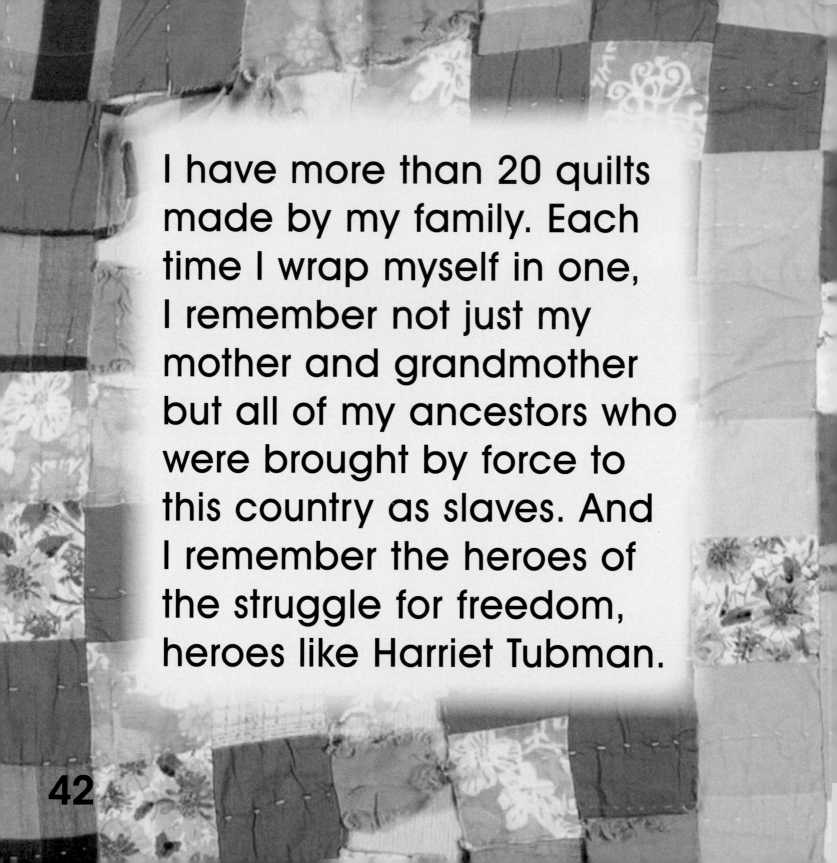

I have more than 20 quilts made by my family. Each time I wrap myself in one, I remember not just my mother and grandmother but all of my ancestors who were brought by force to this country as slaves. And I remember the heroes of the struggle for freedom, heroes like Harriet Tubman.

43

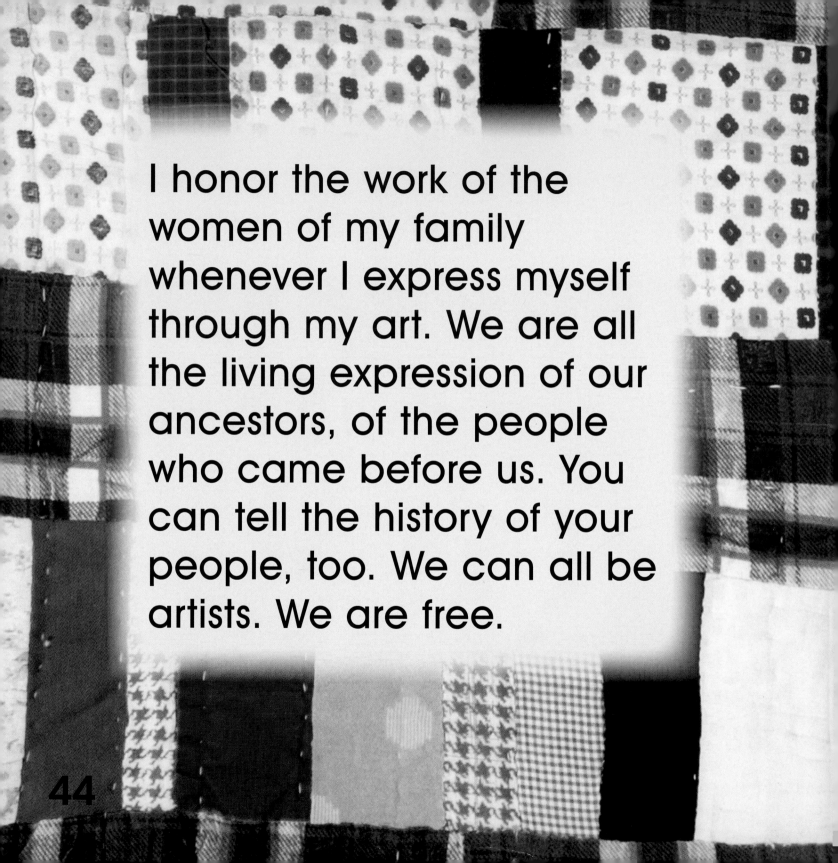

I honor the work of the women of my family whenever I express myself through my art. We are all the living expression of our ancestors, of the people who came before us. You can tell the history of your people, too. We can all be artists. We are free.

44

Born in Birmingham, Alabama, Lorenzo Pace spent his adolescence in Chicago, Illinois. He received his BFA and MFA degrees from the School of the Art Institute of Chicago and his doctorate in art education and administration from Illinois State University in Normal, Illinois. Working with a diversity of objects and materials, Lorenzo has exhibited his sculpture and installations and presented his performance art both nationally and internationally.

In 1992, he was presented with the Keys to the City of Birmingham, Alabama, by Mayor Richard Arrington and Birmingham councilmen Leroy "Tuffy" Bandy and Bernard Kincaid. In 2000, Lorenzo's work was included in "Out of Action: Performance Art 1949–1999," an exhibition of the Museum of Contemporary Art, Tokyo. In the 2008 Olympics in Beijing, Lorenzo represented the United States in an exhibition entitled "One World One Dream" at the Sunshine International Museum of Contemporary Art.

In 2011, investigating his family roots in Tuskegee, Alabama, Lorenzo included as part of a permanent historical marker and art installation a bronze replica of the original slave lock that had held his great-grandfather captive. This installation is at the AME Zion Church in Creek Stand, Alabama, one of the oldest existing slave cemeteries in the United States.

In 2013, Lorenzo's work was also part of a site-specific art installation to honor those people who were taken as slaves from Buea, Cameroon. This installation was part of the "Festival of Sounds, Color, and Arts of Africa" in Douala, Cameroon.

In 2014, Lorenzo was invited to participate in "HistoryMakers," a video oral history of contemporary artists, writers, musicians, actors, and dancers that is now part of the permanent collection at the Library of Congress in Washington, D.C.

Lorenzo currently maintains a studio in Brooklyn, New York. He is the sculptor commissioned to create "Triumph of the Human Spirit" for the African Burial Ground Memorial in Foley Square Park in New York City. He is currently a professor of art at the University of Texas–Rio Grande Valley.

Acknowledgments

The last twenty-five years of continuous personal research of my family tree has been a daunting task, but the end result was to find my family's roots. These books are a major part of this ongoing search, and they are dedicated to many family members and friends. Starting with members of the Clark family who are present today: to Uncle Willie Clark Jr. (1909), Aunt Evelyn Clark (1929), and Elnora Clark Peewee (1914) in Birmingham, Alabama. To members who have passed in the Pace family: my resolute uncle Julian Pace (1911–2006), who presented the original slave lock to me, and to my mother Mary A. Pace (1916–1993) and father Bishop Elder Eddie T. Pace (1909–1991).

These books are also dedicated to my children: Shawn, Ezra, Jalani (the namesake for the first book), and Esperanza. Much respect and thanks to my cousin Shari Williams, director of the Ridge Project of Tuskegee, Alabama, for taking on the difficult task of researching my family tree, starting in Creek Stand, Alabama, the original place of the slave lock of Steve Pace. To all my friends and colleagues who encouraged me to keep going and not to give up on my quest to better understand our collective humanity.

To my little brother Ronald Pace, who is an author himself (*Cane Is Able*, 2012), for his invaluable suggestions and support, which enabled these books to come alive. To the great artist, printmaker, and musician Jose William, who gave me my first art exhibition at the South Side Art Center in Chicago and helped me make my first silk-screen quilt print. To my old Chicago friend and entrepreneur Walter Patrick, who in 1989 first suggested that the publishers review the prototype for *Jalani and the Lock*. Without this introduction, the book might not have come to fruition.

To my colleague Professor Leila Hernandez, an excellent graphic designer at the University of Texas–Rio Grande Valley, for her suggestion to use my grandmother's and mother's quilts as part of the visual concept of the Harriet Tubman volume. To Chicago impresario and author Tom Burrell (*Brainwashed,* 2004), who believed in me before I believed in myself, praising my early artwork and collecting it to this day. To Cassandra Griffen, photojournalist, for her gracious contribution in allowing me to use her photograph of Birmingham civil rights icon Fred Shuttlesworth.

To my soul mate, former teacher at the School of the Art Institute of Chicago, and author Ronne Hartfield (*Another Way Home*, 2004), who introduced me to African literature and heritage as a young art student. This self-reflection led me to the African symbol "Sankofa" meaning "in order to understand oneself as a person, you must look back at your past to move forward into the future." Therefore, to start this process, I had to go to the Motherland of all humanity, Africa.

All this could not have happened without the help, support, and understanding of one of my dearest friends, Lamine Gueye, and his very special family in Dakar, Senegal, West Africa. My travels there to one of Africa's largest slave castles in Gorée Island have provided me with invaluable information and research on the early slave trade to the Americas.

To the publisher Roger Rosen, who had the courage and vision to tackle some of America's most sensitive topics. His orchestration and sensitivity to the completion of these books have made me keenly aware of what a privilege it was to collaborate with this forward-thinking human being. To Brian Garvey, a wonderful graphic designer who was completely up to the challenge of creatively manipulating the visual concepts of the books. Finally, to my brothers and sisters in the Pace family: Eddie Jr., Lawrence, Michael, Alfonzo, William, Ronald, Dorothy, Mary, Shirley, and my sweet sister-in-law Yvonne. To all our future children and to the visionaries who believe in the essence of humanity, so that we can all live in peace and love, celebrating our differences on this beautiful planet that we all share.

~ Dr. Lorenzo Pace